T0129051

Anaïku

17 Little Pieces to A Puzzle

Nyuka Anaïs Laurent

Order this book online at www.trafford.com
or email orders@trafford.com

Most Trafford titles are also available at major online book retailers.

Print information available on the last page.

ISBN: 978-1-4907-3611-2 (sc)
ISBN: 978-1-4907-3612-9 (e)

Trafford rev. 07/26/2017

North America & international
toll-free: 1 888 232 4444 (USA & Canada)
fax: 812 355 4082

Table of Contents

This collection of haïKu poetry

(in my personal format of 4 lines),

as well as the India ink Serendipity Paintings,

is about seeking, finding, adding branches,

losing life partners, healing and learning to forgive

and accept both one's self and others . . .

So life can then move forward.

Anaïku – An Introduction

Healing takes a remarkably long time. Especially if it is not a disease or a virus that has a known cause or treatment. Especially if there is no doctor to prescribe a panacea or a medication developed specifically for that illness. Especially when it concerns not physical health (except as a possible secondary effect), but emotional well-being, and especially if it is individually and personally undertaken, yet has no visible causes and/or effects. It is never totally clear what to attack on what level, nor if it is healing or mourning that needs to take place.

Grief and mourning do not happen overnight. They are not spontaneous, nor are they in the least automatic. Sometimes it takes years before we allow ourselves the time to enter into this type of mental and emotional mop-up. And we all know that dried, caked, leftovers take a lot longer to scrape off . . .

Sometimes the process is one we are aware of, and at other times, it seems to be on standby for long periods at a time, resurfacing at moments of intense emotional upheaval or when a parallel emotional situation suddenly causes the old scars to throb most painfully. I have discovered that if I avoid the pain it simply sinks beneath the surface momentarily. It is not gone, nor is it forgotten; it is merely temporarily submerged. Difficult to drown something so elusive and so strong that nearly capsized our bark, no?

Expectations have been a deadly and insidious poison in my life. Like most people I make the mistake of believing that my expectations have the potential for coming true. That might be true if I were only dealing with myself and my personal hopes and aspirations. It might be true only for my own skills, objectives and future. It is no longer even a knowledgeable risk when dealing with others, who have the terrible habit of doing/being just the opposite and enjoying it! Most often we are disappointed, or worse, offended because people didn't do what we expected of them. That refusal meant that we weren't in control, as we thought we were, not only of ourselves and our lives, but of the other person and his/her life. It also means that perceptions and perspectives need to be reassessed, and in general, nobody likes that kind of work. Because it means asking ourselves some pretty difficult questions—the very ones we had been avoiding because they hurt.

Falling in love is not particularly unusual. It happens all the time and to the nicest people! It happened to me a number of times as a young woman, and then it Really Happened—it took me by the neck and shook me like a terrier does the rabbit once he's dug his way into its burrow to catch it. In fact, it took me by such surprise and so hard that I lost all sense of proportion and of reality. I was young enough, too young in fact to be able to make an intelligent decision, so I heard the Pied Piper and followed him—no, that's not quite true: I chased him until he played for me! I considered the hunt and chase like a game. Not that it wasn't serious. It was, deadly serious, and I wasn't about to lose my quarry. I wanted him and him alone. For some reason I can not understand, only he would assuage my needs—my "biological clock," I think they call it, was ticking and the cuckoo was egging me on!

Headlong in love means a heady, passion, and one that is difficult to sustain at the same level of intensity for a long period of time. This, of course, means someone is, or two someones are, going to be either hurt or disappointed. Generally it is the more romantic of the two partners. When both are sentimental, romantic and artistic in nature, it is an accident waiting to happen, a time bomb waiting to explode.

"If I had been / done" is the breakfast staple of deluded champions. I found myself particularly fond of it for a number of years. They say that hindsight is 20/20. Personally, I find this is true only if one is willing to look at things head-on and objectively, not the easiest thing to do when one is emotionally involved. And so, being weak and not liking confrontation, even with myself, I set whole chunks of unpleasantness aside, telling myself that "Now isn't the time," that I needed to "get over it" or to step back far enough to get a better perspective. But when the wound throbs and refuses to heal, when it begins to ooze pus and turn a livid red, then we know that we've got an infection, that we're in serious trouble and we've got to lance that sucker or it's going to get us in the end!

Healing begins when we stop playing games with ourselves. It begins when we start dealing with the issues. In certain cases it's losing someone we loved. Losing a loved one is just that, losing the person. It does not necessarily mean that the person dies. What it means is that we, personally, have lost someone who was central to our life in every way and influenced it directly. Let's tell it like it was - the bottom fell out of our world! So, healing means that we are allowing ourselves to look at the problem from our personal point of view. We've stopped justifying for whomever, ourselves or the other party. If there is pain then we need to cope with it. Because if we don't, it's going to poison our life for a long time. It may even prevent us from ever getting well enough to move on to other things or other people. We need to grieve, just the same as if we had lost someone to death. They aren't coming back, and even if they did, would we let them, if it provoked more pain?

How often is true forgiveness extended? More often than not, we accept the other back because we think we are strong enough now to do so on **our** terms—in other words, we are starting all over again with the same power kick about who's in charge. It's self-defeating. Programmed self-defeat, just to prove we were right to have left or to have asked for that divorce, etc. It's rather pitiful, and more than sad that we deceive ourselves to such an extent. It's also a double waste of time because we pile more pain (salt) on the wound, and during that time we aren't going anywhere positive.

Honesty. We need to be honest with ourselves. We need to accept the fact that certain feelings that we tell our kids not to have are the very ones we ourselves are feeling—just or unjust—pleasant or unpleasant. Whatever the case, we need to learn to be open and accept the fact that the pain is keeping us from being happy, from moving on, from allowing ourselves the luxury of unlocking all those flood gates and draining the swamp that is serving as a lovely little home for malaria-carrying mosquitoes.

Coming to grips with the need to forgive ourselves for not being omnipotent or omniscient is not easy. Listen to yourself: "I should have known . . ." Hardly pertinent, but it does the trick for self flagellation! And our first reaction is often that need to take on all the guilt involved—it's my fault; I should have done this or that; If only I hadn't; why didn't I? All those questions that we ask ourselves that merely stick our heads in the sand and smother our grief for the moment . . . In fact, the foundations of our lives have been shaken! We're in bad shape here! The person on whom we counted walked out . . . or someone else walked in and took our place. That's one hell of a kicker, now isn't it? Our egos are sadly bruised and frankly, there aren't many of us who look good in that particular combination of brownish yellow mixed with purple!

For every person whose self-image is tarnished, tattered or torn to shreds there is that famous equal and opposing action that takes over and starts us on the spiral of hurt and be hurt that is so useless and devastating. What it takes each of us to wake up to that reality is particular to each individual. It may be a word spoken by a child ("Daddy/Mommy, you're hurting me"). It may be a doctor who tells you that you need to get help because you're going to all kinds of lengths to do away with yourself, and "that ain't healthy!" Whatever the trigger, we need to find it before we can even begin to be honest with ourselves about what is provoking our feelings and behaviour.

Hate.
Now that is a word we despise. Cute. We're playing games with words—again. We do it all the time. Words are so much nicer, easier to manipulate. They don't hurt as much either. However, in this case, we are overwhelmed by this terrible feeling. It is not a word, disinfected, sterilized, cleansed of all the gut-spilling and the gory, vomit-filled guilt that go with it. Despite spending hours drilling our kids about the negativity, the absurdity of wasting our energy on such a futile and draining feeling, we have given in to it. Say it—we hate.

If we listened to our preaching, as we sometimes do, even as we are spewing it, turning-the-other-cheek love is so much better, healthier. It moves in the right direction, it generates a minimum of forgiveness that is the first step in healing. That is certainly true, but that kind of love doesn't stop the hurting, doesn't repair the mutilated sense of self that cries out for revenge, that lashes out without even checking to see if the victim of the assault is the one it is destined for.

In the beginning, we are not lucid. We don't "see" what we are doing. We hurt, and we want to inflict pain in direct response. This is how we feel in the beginning. And it's in the beginning that we have these deep, overpowering feelings that we need to get rid of before they eat us alive, before they take a toll so high that we see no issue that is acceptable, and when we start doing things for which we are no longer truly responsible, the over-the-edge act that we are incapable of analyzing logically. This reaction is called self-preservation, I believe. It's something as simple and basic as that.

When we learn to accept the fact that we, even we, can actually hate someone, then we are on the way to stopping the devastation of that emotion, while at the same time making room for, allowing ourselves to feel something else that might just make us happy(ier?)

Blame. We love it. After that first self-deprecating reaction, we do everything we can to give it to somebody else! We love to lay the blame on their capable broad shoulders. "It's your fault." We are so frail. "It's your fault." We couldn't possibly take it . . . it's too heavy a load. "It's your fault." Taking responsibility for our actions and feelings is ever so hard. "It's your fault."

After all, how can we justify certain things that we did or said or felt? "It's your fault." We are often ashamed of what took place, and sometimes, but not always (as in a case of rape, for example), with some reason. "It's your fault." Perhaps we are not totally to blame, but enough so that it's unpleasant to contemplate it . . . and the direct consequences. "It's your fault." It's so much easier to blame someone else for what we did and are now feeling.

So it becomes a litany that we start believing. But to do so is to prolong the agony. So, as I was saying, it's time to believe that it is okay to have been wrong (even partially) and to say "I'm sorry" to oneself and the other injured party. Make no mistake, there are always at least two, if not more, involved (take the kids, or parents in the middle, as leverage or emotional blackmail . . .) and who are also hurting. "I'm sorry" goes a long way to patching up that wound.

Deaf. Sometimes it's hard to tell someone who is "deaf" what we are trying to do. The cleansing process isn't part of their vocabulary, or in the realm of their understanding. And they don't necessarily want to hear about it, not from us. They refuse, in fact. Scepticism and downright disbelief follow the silence at the other end of the line. But what is more important is our ability to say (and mean what we say) that we were responsible for part of what went wrong. It is the first step in the healing process, taking our share of what happened.

Habits dictate that we don't like feeling guilty, and we may not push on to the end of our self-analysis if we think we are really guilty for what took place. If this is the case, we may not truly benefit from what we have done up to that point either. So, however long it takes, however many times we start and stop, and start over

again, whatever the means we have to find to be able to screw up our courage and continue, we need to find them

How long? Until we can say that the knee-jerk reaction, the brain-washing tip off, the sudden Pavlovian button-pusher is no longer going to get the automatic response it used to get. We can take a breather at that point and consolidate. Then we need to start all over again until we really clear out all the old garbage. Rather like the computer that asks us to wait until all the e-mail files have been checked for any hidden, bugged messages . . . We need to make sure that we give ourselves every chance for the final results to turn out as we wished, until our goals are achieved and we can start breathing again. Did you realize that you had been holding your breath all this time? Well, in a certain way, we do, each and every time we have to put forth serious effort.

And there's no doubting that this process requires putting forth serious effort.

I am blessed. Over the years, my children have each had the patience to provide me with a painting, a drawing that spoke to and of me at just the right moment, a listening ear, a loving presence, and more than once allowed me to share their safe haven, at the expense of their privacy, so I could begin my healing process again and again. And since we are an international family, living in a number of different countries, that sometimes meant an abrupt, impromptu flight across oceans with little warning . . . Many Thanks to you! My thanks also to your life mates, for their patience, understanding and welcome.

Today I can honestly say that although it has been a long hard road, I am nearly well again. As I said before, part of what helped me the most is the compassion and love my children unerringly and altruistically gave me throughout the process.

But part of it is also my insatiable appetite for expressing myself through poetry or short stories. No one can contradict me when I am writing. No one knows but I if what I am writing is real, honest and sincere, or if it is all hogwash. But I ask myself, what is the point if I am not honest with myself? It doesn't usually work unless we are, so if we aren't, we are punishing ourselves once again and that is self-defeating. Reruns are not my cup of tea, even though I do have a tendency to prolong a gig if it's getting enough press!

Healing through poetry and art. What you have

in front of you is the result of over 10 years of soul-searching to try to understand and thoroughly analyse past reactions and emotions. It is my personal shrink. It is also my way of sharing my findings with a public who may have similar problems but not be able to express them. So, I am your mouth; I am your tongue. I am your barricade of teeth against which your tongue strikes when it forms those hard sounds that need to be said . . . I hope that my findings, not all of which are happy, romantic little gems of wisdom, will be useful to you, and maybe even bring you catharsis. If so, then I have healed not only myself, but started others on their search for inner acceptance as well, and I am content.

I welcome and thank you for any comments. Please write them to my e-mail address at anais@montmollin.ch. I truly hope this series of 17-syllable poems will allow you to start your own process of healing, and that the unusual line organization (normally a Japanese haiku is 5 / 7/ 5 syllables, but I have taken the liberty of using 4 lines) will encourage you to take some liberties and dip your quill into your feelings, as well. Poetry is one Mother of a healer! Enjoy the release it gives you . . . some blank areas have been left for your creative, positive feedback to yourselves.

Dedication

This collection of poems is dedicated to my children, Lise, Sébastien and Thierry, for the huge part they have played in allowing me to heal myself.

The generosity of spirit and the love they have constantly shown me created an environment that was propitious to this long and oftentimes drawn out process.

I wish to thank you for your patience and compassion, your understanding and ability to remain non judgmental.

And above all, my thanks for your loving support.

I also wish to thank Kim Fyock and Esther Davidowitz for their belief in my writing capacities. Acknowledgement is so important to the ego-bolstering required to make public such a personal work.

Part I

Before We Were Two

Before we were two,
The hunt was all.
The question was,
Who'd capture whom?

Lazy afternoons,
Stoop – sitting:
Checking out firm tushies
Hugged by jeans.

Taffeta snicks,
Crushed velvet murmurs;
Silk whispers:
Tempting foreplay sounds.

Cool arrogance.
Gold-adorned Nubian
On the make,
Check'n out chicks.

He struts and preens.
All slick and sheen,
Polished up for
A hot night on town.

Gonnagitme
Awhitechickee,
Makerworkfirme
Giteven.

A dancer floats by,
A glide for a walk:
Eager eyes trace curves,
Tongues lick lips.

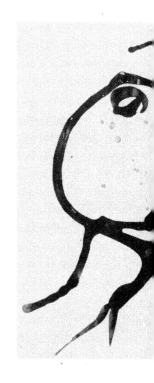

Blond god prances by,
No flies on him!
No woman's hands either;
Such waste.

Café lady asks
Pedestrian male:
"Join me?"
"Sorry, got a wife."

Watering holes
Often spawn
Mosquito brains,
Pesky social gnats.

Gold teeth smile
Invitingly;
Velvet hand makes
A pass – duck, girl!

Barman counsels
"Let it pass.
He don't mean nothin';
Liquor makes men bold."

She nods sagely,
Plays dumb,
Misunderstands innuendos:
Smart bimbo!

Women listen
To men's tall tales,
Boost frail egos,
A thankless task.

Saint Valentine
Is a hypocrite:
He preaches love
But shoots us down.

Who would be
So foolish as to
Give up freedom
To be bound by love?

For cornflower eyes
What would one not do?
For waving grain
Of hips, all.

Giving up
One night stands
For every night forever
Scares the shit out!

Close enough to touch;
Wary enough
To be scared;
Bugle blows "Retreat!"

So many questions,
So few answers
given;
Personal protection.

Do you even know
You're withholding
info?
Honesty's needed!

Love knots tighten
To hangman's noose:
Why not half-hitch,
Or give him the slip?

Burning appetites
Sear the flesh
Then woof it down
Like tender meat.

Fetishes fetter
With bonds of silk,
Horsehair whips
And jewelled manacles.

Between plunder and passion,
Rapine and rapture,
Lies love's
Thin line.

Not always pretty,
Love beads on upper lips,
Drops on crumpled sheets,
Drowns.

You seek me out
In dreams, in sleep;
We touch, you smile
And then roll over.

Click, click . . . click!
There it is again,
That click that signifies
We two click!

Two auras embrace
Like morning glory
Up twine.
First love-blossoms bloom.

Love's alchemy
Achieves miracles.
Mere chemistry
Cannot fuse souls.

Satin sheets slip
From satin thighs.
Whale bones creak.
Moby Dick dives then spouts.

After love
Old bones unfold stiffly:
Our minds more used
To straddling.

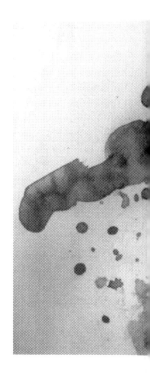

Second time around
Is not
A repeat,
But variable interest.

You carry me
Over thresholds
Of past loves
With infinite patience.

Please leave behind
Your yellow roses.
Inconstancy
Is not my thing . . .

I want to;
I'll try to:
The only promises
I can offer now.

Part IIa

Tying Knots
in Macramour

Sharing common interests
Brings much more
Than simple joy;
It ties tight knots.

Silken threads
Woven together
In love's tapestry
Bind us as one.

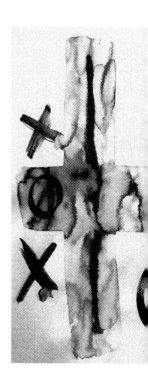

Joined hands pledged
Troths with rings of gold,
But bound our lives
By love's silver cords.

Marriage is a quest
To find the Grail
Of understanding
And of love.

How would you have me
Love you, hard or soft?
No, with empathy
And romance.

Young love is feckless,
Daring all;
Mature love walks softly,
Sharing space.

We banked
Personal needs
And stoked passion's fire.
Will we go up in smoke?

The world intrudes
Like waves upon
Our castle. Did we
Build strong enough?

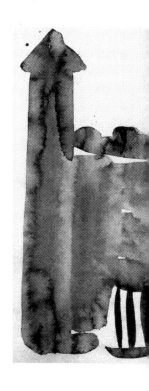

Modern science
Frees today's couples
To choose when
And how many. Why?

We ploughed the fields
But let our seed lie
Dormant, wrapped
In condom cocoons.

Before we share
Our space with kids,
We should make sure
It is secure.

Building a nest
Seems paramount
To young lovers;
More than communing.

Mindful of his duty,
He works long hours
To provide.
Alone, she weeps.

Stolen moments
On forest paths
Bring relief from stress
On career paths.

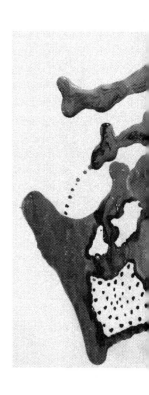

Narcissus saw his
Mirrored self and threw
Caution to the wind:
We, too.

You dampen my ardour
With sweet love dew.
Will it grow
New shoots of you?

I quicken
To rotundity.
Will it fulfil,
As well as fill me?

In Love's name
You weeded my plot,
Stomping sweet flowers
Of chaos out.

Where are all the titbits
You used to feed me
To nurture love?
I starve . . .

Hold me tight,
You warm me;
Hold me too tight,
I suffocate. Let go!.

In the garden of my heart
Children bloomed,
Spread like weeds
And choked him out.

Upstaged by kids,
The has-been husband
Seeks spot lights
In another's eyes.

Finding acceptance
Elsewhere,
He hides his guilt,
Rediscovers True Love.

A single look
Of scorn chastises:
Understanding dies,
Silence clots.

Logic and Art
Are difficult bedmates.
I changed to please
And lost you.

Clinging, I choke
"I'm addicted to you!
Just one more toke
Before you go . . ."

You must have been
A black belt expert:
This jealous choke hold
Strangles love!

Daily trysts for honor
Find us lacking,
Lances broken
On windmills.

Reconstructing bridges
Is far harder
Than burning them
All to Hell.

Parched mouth, gritty words,
Sirocco sighs
Blister me with his scorn:
Love dies.

You move your pawns,
Anger to Pain;
I prefer to check-mate
King instead.

If words were precious
We'd treasure them,
And measure
Each more carefully.

The ship of love
Lies rudderless;
Tatters of hope
Flap in the wind.

Family guy lines
Stay, coerce, fray.
They could be spliced
To bind us.

Fingertips bleed
From too often darning
The threadbare
Garment of love.

Clouds of obscenities
Fly overhead.
I duck
And run for home.

War worn, we bled
From every scar,
And clutched at
Empty air for comfort.

When all is said,
What kills
A relationship is
What is left unsaid.

"Get a life,"
He quipped sarcastically.
And so I did:
I got divorced.

When you leave,
Close the door gently,
As once you did
When you entered here.

Waiting, waiting
Sitting and waiting.
My ship comes in,
Its holds empty.

Scars benign
Hide deadly shrapnel:
Shards of memory
Working heartward.

Autumn moon,
Amber hair;
Am I cursed to see her
Everywhere?

We mortals
Merely love.
Fireflies go nova
In their brief courtship.

Longings
For what I do not have,
For what I once did,
Bring endless grief.

Withering buds fall.
Rafter-dried,
Hung upside-down,
Fleeting colors saved.

Hit buttons,
Redesign and refresh
Internal views;
Changing paradigms.

Phoenix, bright-eyes,
Rises anew
From love's ashes:
Hope from despair.

As bleeding tides ebb,
Fresh footprints appear,
Etch the sands
Of my beached heart.

I pray they will remain
Even after
High tides
retire.

Sweet amnesia,
House of dreams
And flights of fantasy.
Why rewrite?

Part IIb

Tying Knots
in Macramour

A ripe melon,
I bear our first.
You marvel:
It's a World Premier!

Family ties, warm quilts
Upon rope beds,
Sleep tight, child,
Secure in love. .

Children, addictions mine!
Hooked on their love,
I keep wanting more,
Like sweets.

Three branches, ours.
Each one bears
A different fruit:
Two nations' grafted genes.

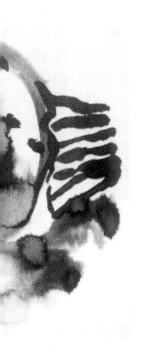

Child in shallows
Catches minnows
In pink undies:
Tickling trout!

Naked boy climbs
Stairs on all-fours,
Points at five-legged shadow
And crows!

Elder son perches
On stools; top heavy,
He falls square on
Rock targets.

Jealous squabbles
For attention
Lead to first theft . . .
Beware sweet smiles!

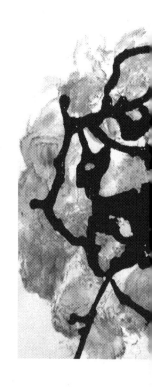

Flip sides of a coin,
Years apart,
Twins in nature;
So too, their love / hate.

These agonies,
Will also pass:
Bitter battles
For Identity.

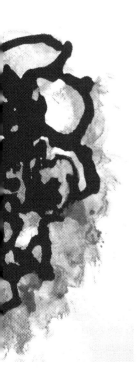

After the squabbles
Comes mass exodus,
Each intent
On finding self.

Who will fill
This silent void
Of toddlers' feet
And cries of "Mommy, please!"

However different
As they mature,
One trait's the same:
Their stubborn pride!

The rapids of time
Flow too swiftly:
Daddy's kitten
Becomes a cat!

Forgiveness for slights
Is too much to ask
Of teenager
Wounded pride.

Yesterday's shoes grow
Too small and pinch,
Just like
Father / son outings do.

Daughter,
Goddess incarnate,
Beauty and grace balance
Youth's righteous rage!

Aspiring actress
Rehearses roles,
Strives for emotion,
Fools herself.

Sphinx, your name
Is Mother! Your silent
"Guilty" judgments
Entomb my hopes!

Bright-eyed scholar
Requires no teacher
To know the rewards
Of knowledge.

Dad's displeased:
Younger son's half-smile
Wobbles like jello.
Instant desert.

When fathers and sons
No longer speak
Mothers often
Become scapegoats.

Frustrated ideals
Turn turgid,
Then break out
In rude belligerence.

Free fall flights
Into despair
Open exit doors
Leading to sheer Hell.

Trust must be earned.
What, like allowance?
No, like respect
And honesty.

If elder son's
Straight forward truth
Were any sharper
It would kill us both.

If parents are
An Enigma to kids,
Then children are
Beastie Boys!

Mémé pursed her lips.
Generations of children
Fell silent
And quailed!

Clothes, shoes,
Jewelry and make-up
Disappear. Nothing's
Sacred to kids!

In open revolt,
Children attack
The foundations of
The Establishment.

Thunderheads loom,
Lightening storms rage:
Teen tantrums
Ravage my countryside!

He smiles; I, too, sadly,
Knowing the truce
Is short-lived.
He needs the car!

Who sits by the phone
More than kids do?
Parents waiting
For that call.

Passive aggressive,
He waits his chance
To nip Achilles' heel,
Then sneers . . .

Where we crusaded,
Apathy reigns.
Are adults to blame
That life sucks?

As baby steps progress
To giant steps
She steps out
Of our lives.

A graceful model,
A prima on stage;
Mothers live
Vicariously.

Reality check:
A pinch in time
May keep a line
From my son's nose.

Booze, pills or smak,
Spikes, lines or crack:
Addictions set
Death's place at table.

Alcohol abuse,
Pot in home-made
water pipes;
I fear for my son.

Summer beer parties.
Peer pressure taunts
The feeble.
"Drink 'til you drop, Kid!"

Terror calls:
All night vigil
By stark white bed
Makes scared and wiser child.

Children, immortals all.
Worlds rise and fall,
Not they.
"Prometheus, I."

The Sacristy of Self
Must extend
Sanctuary to
One's offspring. .

Old age slows us down.
Thickens blood
And points of view,
Makes us near-sighted.

Phoenix,
He rises, exchanging
Blanket hatred,
For music and art.

Like a flower,
Self-assurance
Must be nurtured,
Or else it will wilt.

You chose my friends;
You chose my lovers:
You'd choose my husband.
What's left, Mom?

Too late we discover,
Interference
Is best run
By peer tacklers.

Self-doubt assails:
Could we have done
A better job?
Is this déjà vu?

Hello, Mother!
Have you come back
In me to repeat
The past?

Lit by flame, bright sparks
Consumed by passion,
Died to coals
That fused frayed ends.

Part III

Frayed Ends

With age,
Distance and freedom,
All children become
Less vitriolic.

Doors once slammed
In haste to escape
Are cracked open
For practical needs. . .

Brothers and sisters
Grow up to relate,
Discover parents
Once loved.

Children are said
To bind solid couples;
Love's loose ends
Sometimes just fray.

After the fall,
So little grace
Is left, we stumble
Even on words.

You see it your way,
I see it mine,
No one's to blame
It didn't work.

Crumpled, like a wad
Of paper on the floor,
I awaited
numbness.

Logic dictates
That anger and pain
Will subside:
Hearts still cry in grief.

I can not tell
Your version;
Analyzing my own
Nearly killed me.

I ask myself,
When did who had
The upper hand
Become so crucial?

How can we atone
For guilt we refuse
To acknowledge
As our own?

Man's bitterness
Is proportional to
The sum of
Dashed illusions.

Letting go
Is so much harder
Than clinging to
The known pain of loss.

Haunted eyes,
Deep-circled by
Sleepless nights,
Seek pillow comfort; find none.

Endless heart ache:
Longings for him
I no longer hold,
Hold tight to me.

Memories stalk me
In the night,
Replace his foot step
On the stairs.

Once, before, artful fingers
Traced my spine,
Painted goose bumps . . .
Now, cold does.

Stretched thin,
Constant agonizing
Over might-have-beens,
A torture rack.

Identities lost
In the nebulous "WE"
Condense:
My tears form rain.

Sad refrains
Replayed time and again:
Sour notes skewed
Our symphony.

Bitterness is bile
Rising daily
To the gorge:
Mourning sickness.

Curious chemistry:
Sands that filled
Love's hour glass
Sift down to hate.

Friends stop by to grieve,
Then tip toe out,
As if this were
A funeral.

Unable to love both,
Friends choose sides,
Battle ranks are formed,
Numbers swelled.

Divorce is clan war:
Cause forgotten,
Hate sustains
Hit and run tactics.

With deadly accuracy
We both count coup,
As if pain
Could redeem.

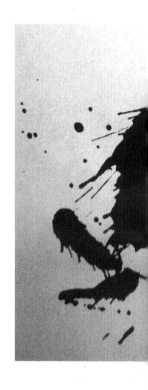

After the holocaust,
Census-takers count
Our gruesome
Casualties.

Tragedy.
An entire family
Gone MIA
In divorce courts.

We edit life's script
With such ease
We should have been
T.V. Soap writers.

Within a year,
You find a mate
To fill the void.
I lick countless wounds.

No master now, I've shed
My band of gold.
Clipped wings maimed,
I still can't fly.

Basic needs:
Love, acceptance.
At forty,
Infantile paralysis.

Practical needs
Wean me from
The teat of Romance.
Withdrawal pangs.

Assuming problems
I hoped never
To shoulder,
I stoop under strain.

A lazy Susan,
Life's carousel
Breaks down:
Excess baggage hang-ups.

Prone to
Submissive behaviour:
Not acting,
I was acted upon.

Self-abuse brings
Self-defeat.
Sooner or later
We'll pick ourselves up.

Halter and lead rope
Set aside,
I'm getting used
To independence.

I'll not saddle
Myself with another
Rodeo rider:
Burrs scratch!

Once a comfort,
Four walls contract
To become a
Celibate monk cell.

Territorial markers,
Stone walls crumble
With age,
Invite trespass.

Solitude is nearly
As heavy as
The lead in my ass!
Get out!!!

Sewn together
By a basting stitch,
Highway seams beckon
Like zippers.

Separated parents
Make life hard:
Children fill the voids
With new strengths.

Single parents
Do the best they can,
But one role model
Can't play two.

Old adages are true:
One must let go
To see them
Return freely.

Tender moments:
Mother – daughter talk
Shares grief, pain, joy,
Recreates bonds.

They hated the country
To which we moved:
Today, they return
With joy.

Empty nest, silence filled.
Offspring visit,
Their mates in tow . . .
Fledglings soon?

Cycles turn.
I tremble at the thought
That you'll rewrite
Our history.

There was passion,
Then love, then pain.
Like every parent
I wish you more.

Life goes on.
My children, generous,
Wish me both
Love and happiness.

May you
Who gave me joy
As I watched you grow
Find all you seek from life.

Useless to tell you
Not to make the same
Mistakes:
Your life is **YOUR** life.

Epilogue and Appendices

Dear ones,
May life treat you well;
Grant you
Shelter from ugliness
Strength to overcome
And love to bring you joy.

India ink paintings

Printed in the United States
By Bookmasters